Cathy Williams, Buffalo Soldier

CATHY WILLIAMS, BUFFALO SOLDIER

By Sharon Solomon
Illustrated by Doreen Lorenzetti

To Corey and Victoria,
I hope you are inspired
by Cathy's true story!
Sharon Solomon

PELICAN PUBLISHING COMPANY
GRETNA 2010

*To Carolyn Briles, Joseph Inbar, Ann Richards, and
Carol Ann Stanger for their unwavering support and
encouragement—S.S.*

*Special thanks to Sharon Solomon, dear friends and family,
and my children, Christopher, Jonathan, and Cheyanna—D.L.*

Copyright © 2010
By Sharon Solomon

Illustrations copyright © 2010
By Doreen Lorenzetti

Library of Congress Cataloging-in-Publication Data

Solomon, Sharon K.
  Cathy Williams, Buffalo Soldier / Sharon Solomon ; illustrated by
Doreen Lorenzetti.
    p. cm.
  Includes bibliographical references.
  ISBN 978-1-58980-801-0 (hardcover : alk. paper) 1. Williams, Cathy,
b. 1844—Juvenile literature. 2. African American women—Biography—
Juvenile literature. 3. African Americans—Biography—Juvenile
literature. 4. Women slaves—Missouri—Independence—Biography—
Juvenile literature. 5. Women soldiers—West (U.S.)—Biography—
Juvenile literature. 6. False personation—Case studies—Juvenile
literature. 7. African American soldiers—West (U.S.)—Biography—
Juvenile literature. 8. United States. Army—African American troops—
History—19th century—Juvenile literature. 9. Frontier and pioneer
life—West (U.S.)—Juvenile literature. I. Lorenzetti, Doreen, ill. II. Title.
  E185.97.W694S68 2010
  978'.02092—dc22
  [B]
                                        2010012685

∞ ©

Printed in Singapore
Published by Pelican Publishing Company, Inc.
1000 Burmaster Street, Gretna, Louisiana 70053

Cathy Williams was born in 1844. Although her father was a free man, her mother was a slave, making Cathy a slave. In 1848, when she was four years old, Cathy and her mother were sold to Mr. William Johnson near Jefferson City, Missouri. Cathy never saw her father again.

Bill of Sale

Negro woman about twenty years of age plus female offspring age four years purchased by William Johnson on this tenth day of September in the year of 1848.

Since Cathy and her mother were slaves, they worked in the big house cleaning and doing laundry and were considered property like a chicken or a horse. However, Cathy's life was about to change. In the fall of 1861, the North and South were fighting the Civil War over states' rights and the expansion of slavery.

One day, a group of Union soldiers rode into the Johnson farm and freed all of their slaves. Upon hearing the news, the slaves cried, hugged, and sang with joyous voices. Singing and praying were the only ways for slaves to use their voices.

Cathy and her mother soon set out for Jefferson City. Union soldiers occupied the city, setting up camp and handing out food to freed slaves who were homeless. Once there, the pair wandered the streets looking for jobs. They had never learned to read or write, so it was hard to find work.

Without warning, Cathy was taken by the Union army. The law allowed the army to take former slaves as contraband and force them to work as military support for very little pay. Cathy did not want to go. That would be the last time Cathy ever saw her mama.

Cathy was seventeen years old when she was assigned to do laundry for the officers of the Eighth Indiana Volunteer Infantry, which was under the command of Colonel William Plummer Benton. For three and a half years, Cathy and the other workers walked alongside the Eighth Indiana as the soldiers marched hundreds of miles across the South.

The first action Cathy experienced was the Battle of Pea Ridge, Arkansas, in March of 1862. The sounds of thundering cannons and screaming shells overhead frightened her. She hid in her tent, singing songs and prayers that reminded her of her mama.

The following year, Cathy was surprised when Colonel Benton sent her to Little Rock, Arkansas, to learn how to cook. When she returned to her regiment, she did laundry and cooked for the officers.

The Civil War went on much longer than either side thought it would. Cathy did not know when she would return to Missouri. At night, she prayed that her mother was well. She prayed in the daytime when they marched to New Orleans. She prayed when she saw the soldiers burning cotton in Shreveport.

In 1864, the Eighth Indiana was assigned to Virginia. They traveled by steamboat up the Atlantic Ocean to Washington, D.C. Cathy thought that her nation's capital was beautiful.

Cathy and her regiment marched over hills and streams until they reached the beautiful Shenandoah Valley.

Suddenly Cathy was assigned to cook for General Philip Sheridan's headquarters at the Belle Grove House in Middletown, Virginia. She missed her friends at the Eighth Indiana and hoped to return to them soon.

Throughout the war, the Confederacy sent armies through the Shenandoah Valley in an attempt to invade Washington, D.C. On October 19, 1864, while General Sheridan was away, Lieutenant General Jubal Early launched a surprise Confederate attack, causing the Union soldiers to run into the hills. Cathy ran for cover and hid in a hayloft for two days until the fighting was over. The ground shook, and the gunfire sounded as fierce as a thunderstorm. When General Sheridan returned from Winchester, Virginia, he ordered his men to attack the Rebels. Early and his soldiers were defeated at Cedar Creek and finally left the Shenandoah Valley forever.

When the Civil War was finally over in 1865, Cathy returned to Missouri to look for her mother. Cathy was working at the Jefferson Army Barracks when she met her cousin and his friend. They did not know her mother's whereabouts. Cathy felt so alone, but she was comfortable being around the soldiers.

Cathy's cousin and his friend told Cathy that they were joining the army to fight in the Indian Wars. Congress had passed the Act to Increase and Fix the Military Peace Establishment of the United States on July 28, 1866, which allowed black men to enlist in the United States Army. And that gave Cathy an idea.

She knew that she was tall and strong, and she wanted to earn thirteen dollars a month. She wanted to save money and use it for her future. Therefore, Cathy cut her hair short and dressed in men's clothing. She told the army doctor that her name was William Cathay. She looked so much like a man that she fooled them and enlisted!

That is how Cathy Williams became the first female Buffalo Soldier. The Indians called the black soldiers "Buffalo Soldiers" because their hair was curly like buffalo hair.

Cathy's regiment marched across Missouri to Colorado and New Mexico. Cathy was a good soldier. She learned to shoot a musket and carried it while on guard duty. She helped protect the settlers from robbers and Indians. Her first view of the Rocky Mountains was breathtaking, and she fell in love with the West. She told herself some day she would live there.

Living so close together in the barracks made it easy for soldiers to catch diseases from one another, and, unfortunately, Cathy fell ill several times during her military service. The Buffalo Soldiers had poor food and water supplies. When Cathy was hospitalized with smallpox, she kept herself covered up, afraid the doctors would discover her secret. Soon she rejoined her company, but got sick again. Eventually, Cathy grew tired of army life and finally stopped hiding her female identity. She was discharged from the army in 1868.

Cathy had saved her military earnings, so she had money to move out West. First she settled in Raton, New Mexico, and then in Pueblo, Colorado. Cathy said, "I got a good sewing machine and got washing to do and clothes to make. I know I can make my own living and be independent."

Cathy started a laundry business and bought a wagon and a team of horses. People called her Miss Kate. Eventually, Cathy settled in Trinidad, Colorado, where she found work and received land from the government near the train depot. There she built a small adobe home with a view of the golden Rocky Mountains.

Land Grant

Miss Kate's Laundr

Cathy was no longer a slave or a house girl. She was no longer a Civil War washwoman or cook. She was no longer a Buffalo Soldier. She was free and proud. She was finding her own voice in a place where no slaves had ever walked.

Afterword

In April 1891, Cathy Williams applied for disability
from the United States Army, but it was denied. She was
in poor health when the army doctor examined her. Cathy
had had some toes amputated and was walking with two
canes. Her enlistment papers are in the National Archives
in Washington, D.C.; however, there are no records
indicating when or where she died. Some sources claim
she lived to age eighty-two, but no documentation exists
showing Cathy living in Trinidad or Pueblo in the 1920s.

Bibliography

Allen, Thomas B. *The Blue and the Gray*. Washington,
   D.C.: National Geographic Society, 1992.
Cox, Clinton. *The Forgotten Heroes: The Story of the
   Buffalo Soldiers*. New York: Scholastic Press, 1993.
Davis, Kenneth C. *Don't Know Much about the Civil War:
   Everything You Need to Know about America's Greatest
   Conflict but Never Learned*. New York: William Morrow,
   1996.
Mitchell, Reid. *Civil War Soldiers*. New York: Simon and
   Schuster, 1989.
Tucker, Phillip Thomas. *Cathy Williams: From Slave to
   Female Buffalo Soldier*. Mechanicsburg, PA: Stackpole
   Books, 2002.
Willard, Tom. *Buffalo Soldiers*. New York: Forge
   Publishing, 1996.